D1488085

201

Ways to Deal With Difficult People

A Quick-Tip Survival Guide

ALAN AXELROD & JIM HOLTJE

MJF BOOKS
NEW YORK

Published by MJF Books
Fine Communications
Two Lincoln Square
60 West 66th Street
New York, NY 10023

201 Ways to Deal With Difficult People
LC Control Number 01-130249
ISBN 1-56731-463-5

Manufactured in the United States of America on acid-free paper ∞

MJF Books and the MJF colophon are trademarks of Fine Creative Media, Inc.

BG   10 9 8 7 6 5 4 3 2 1

Other Quick-Tip Survival Guides:

201 Ways to Manage Your Time Better
201 Ways to Say No Gracefully and Effectively

CONTENTS

Quick Start ix

You Are Not Alone 1

Bosses from Hell 7

Colleagues from Purgatory 17

Employees from Hunger 25

Clients from New York 33

Silencing a Screamer 41

Riposting Rudeness 47

Outmaneuvering Schemers 55

Navigating the Egotist's World 61

Care and Feeding of Passive-Aggressive People 67

Lazy No More 75

Beating Up Bullies 83

Crushing Constant Critics 91

Puncturing Perfectionists 97

Outmanipulating the Manipulative 105

Surviving the Stubborn 113

Neutralizing Morale Busters 121

Tackling the Taciturn 129

Functioning with Fault-Finders 137

Creative Venting 145

QUICK START

The folks flipping burgers at the fast-food joint are the last of the 9-to-5ers.
The forty-hour week? In your dreams. Try *sixty hours*. Minimum.

Hours. There aren't enough of them. Succeeding in business has
always been a tough go. These days, it's downright brutal. What do you
need most?

All the help you can get.

What do you need even more?

Time.

The Quick-Tip Survival Guides put the two together, giving you all the
help you need—without taking all the time you have.

Here is a series for today's business reader. A reader pressed by a
hundred demands and pulled in a dozen directions. (Business as usual!)
A reader whose day shoots by in milliseconds, who consumes information
by the megabyte, and who cannot afford the luxury of climbing the
learning curve with the leisurely aid of traditional narrative prose.

Here is a series for today's business reader negotiating today's learning curve. Focusing on the personal and interpersonal skills crucial to working successfully with customers, colleagues, subordinates, and supervisors, the Quick-Tip Survival Guides mine and refine the nuggets of essential business know-how: the time-tested truths, together with savvy from the cutting edge.

201 Ways to Deal with Difficult People looks at real-world situations you face in business every day and provides no-nonsense strategies for turning close encounters of the worst kind into civil, sane, and productive exchanges between you, your subordinates and employees, your colleagues and coworkers, your customers and clients, and your supervisors and bosses.

YOU ARE
NOT ALONE

1. Begin dealing with difficult people by realizing that they really care very little about *you*. Their focus is themselves, *only* themselves. You are a blip on their radar screen—important only if you happen to get in between them and what they want, or if they need you to get something they want. Don't take what they say or do too personally.

2. Difficult people won't change on their own, and, unfortunately, it's not likely that you will be able to change them. Before you let this fact depress you, consider that, because they tend *not* to change, their behavior is usually predictable. While you should not expect too much of difficult people, at least you can thoroughly prepare for encounters with them. While planning your approach won't change a difficult personality, it may very possibly have a positive effect on the outcome of any encounter.

3. You can approach the difficult person with your teeth gritted, determined to have a miserable experience. Or you can try to be as positive as possible. Formulate a strategy. Decide in advance what results you would like to achieve rather than concentrate on negative issues or your bad feelings about the difficult person.

4. Express your feelings. Don't bottle up irritation, outrage, annoyance, or feelings of hurt. If someone offends you, say how you feel. However, avoid accusations. Instead, ask clarifying questions: "I'm not sure I understand what you meant by that remark. Can you explain that to me?"

5. As you should express your feelings, invite others to express theirs. Seek feedback. You need to know how your boss, your colleagues, your subordinates, your customers feel about what's going on or what you are doing. Don't try to guess what someone else is thinking. Ask.

6. Use open-ended questions to inquire about feelings and opinions. Don't coach or limit an answer by offering multiple choices. Avoid, for example: "Tell me, do you like my idea a lot or a little?" Ask instead: "Joe, what do you think about the idea?"

7. In cases of dispute, hold off placing personal blame. Instead, appeal to a higher authority—preferably something totally objective, such as a rule book, a protocol manual, a policies and procedures guide, or some similar source.

8. Keep documentation. This may not only limit or entirely avert disputes with difficult people, it might just save your hide. Movie mogul Samuel Goldwyn once said that "a verbal contact ain't worth the paper it's printed on." Write a memo when you make an assignment. When your boss assigns you a major project, get the specifics in writing. If the assignment is made verbally, send a confirming memo that states the specifics. Get the other person to sign off on it.

9. While documentation is valuable, don't let written memos become substitutes for face-to-face conversations. Deal directly with everyone, difficult people included. It is important to see their body language, to hear the tone of their voice. It is equally important that they see you as fully dimensional human being— not a collection of words on a page or a disembodied voice on the phone.

10. Stay calm. This is simple, bland, obvious advice. Certainly, it is not always easy advice to follow. However, if you can remain calm and courteous, chances are that you will not escalate a difficult situation into an impossible one. Such behavior will also stake out for you the moral high ground, so that, if a difficult person's behavior goes from annoying to unbearable, you may withdraw from the "conversation" with a comment like this: "Mary, I am speaking calmly and civilly to you. I expect the same in return. Please see me when you've calmed down, and we can continue to talk."

11. Practice generosity and graciousness. Nothing confers greater authority and power than treating your enemies as you would your friends. Be wary, but be courteous.

12. Go out of your way to ask difficult people for their opinion and for their help. Getting them to take an interest in you will tend to give them an ownership stake in your projects and your problems. This may do little to change a troublesome personality, but it may well transform how this person behaves toward you and works with you.

13. Keep difficult people in perspective by recognizing that they are in the minority. Focus on your friends and family. Focus on colleagues who are helpful, and on clients with whom it is a pleasure to work. Don't let difficult people become the mote-in-the-eye that clouds your vision.

BOSSES

FROM HELL

14. Without needlessly raising your blood pressure, try to recall some truly awful bosses you've had over your career. You know: the yellers, the screamers, the manipulators, the connivers—the ones who controlled your *paycheck*. We've all had our share. If you have a terrific boss today, congratulations. It makes work a lot easier. If not, read on. Many problem bosses are arrogant—arrogant because they are in a position of power and don't know how to exercise that power effectively. The arrogant boss typically claims your work as his own. One of the best ways to counter this is deliberately to play his game. Don't take the high-handedness personally. Rather, tell him how important he has been in helping advance your career and how you couldn't do what you do without him.

15. Bosses are a special breed. You might be able to get away with telling colleagues honestly how you feel about them, but if you value your job, you will always have to tread lightly with the boss. With a boss who is a nitpicker, lost in details, it is always a good idea to document your work. Consider sending progress memos to let her know exactly what you've done, and what you've got left to finish. Nitpickers thrive on control. Therefore, give them the *feeling* of control. "I thought you'd want an update on the XZY project. To date, we have accomplished the following . . ."

16. If your boss tells you one thing, and then you find out he meant something else, it's important to set the record straight and to do so quickly. Ask him questions that require factual answers— not answers based on perceptions or feelings. "I'm surprised, because you told me our division would be in charge of that account. I wrote that here in my notes of the last meeting." Always be diplomatic, and never seek a confrontation, but do prompt him to own up to his decisions.

17. There's a TV commercial for a popular deodorant that ends with the tag line: "Never let them see you sweat." Good advice. If your boss is of the worst variety—a screamer, say—learn the following techniques fast. When an explosion erupts, many employees feel the need to respond in kind—that is, to yell back. Big mistake. Learn to tune out the worst of the yelling. Most of the time, it's just an emotional outburst that lasts only a few minutes and quickly blows over. The best way to deal with a screaming boss is to refrain from returning fire. Even if you're right, you're wrong. Nudge her toward calm reason, which may begin with your removing yourself—temporarily—from the scene. "I understand you're angry, but we need to look at this rationally. Maybe it's best if I come back later so we can go over this again."

18. The temptation is always there. You know you want to say it: *"You're an idiot. In fact, you're the biggest idiot I've ever worked for."* Boy, that felt good. But it's a good thing you didn't really say it. Unfortunately, as an employee, the deck is stacked against you. The boss can, perhaps, afford to explode, but you cannot. If you feel the pressure building, try this: Count silently to 20 as he fumes and fusses. Don't jump into the fray. If 20 counts aren't enough—if the boss is still bellowing—count to 30 or 60. Give yourself whatever breathing space is required, and let the boss vent while you breathe. Once you stoop to your boss's infantile level, you will lose.

19. If things get bad enough, you might want to talk to the human resources person at your company. Some firms offer mediation and conflict-resolution assistance, which may be useful in settling differences with a difficult boss. Often, this involves working with someone above your boss. Bear in mind that taking your problems to a level above your boss exposes her to scrutiny she does not want. Mediation can resolve a problem, but if it fails to do so—if human resources proves ineffectual—your boss may well bear a grudge and think of you as disloyal. Ponder very carefully before you break this particular egg.

20. Rumor mongers and back stabbers make awful bosses. They typically have an immature streak in them that runs deep and wide. The only way to stop rumors is to confront their source, and if that is your boss, you've got a tough task. "I'm sorry to bring this up, but it's come to my attention that you said the following about me . . . Is this true?" Odds are, if the person is indeed guilty, she will not own up to it. In this case, offer no challenge, but respond with something like: "Good, I'm glad to hear that. I didn't think you'd say something nasty like that." This sends two signals: First, your boss's attempt to throw you off-balance failed, and, second, it indicates that you really do know the source of the rumor. This latter revelation should make your boss uncomfortable enough to think twice the next time she is tempted to start a rumor about you.

21. Be careful what you say to an abusive boss in front of other people. You're at a meeting, and your boss's boss is present. Now both he and you are on stage. Your boss, of course, is far more concerned with how he looks in *his* boss's eyes than how you look. It is probably in your best interest to create an overall favorable impression in order to deprive your boss of any ammunition he might use later. You might have to put on an award-winning acting performance, but it's worth it. Never give your boss the chance to say, "You made me look like a fool in there!" Those could be the last words you ever hear from him.

22. Be more proactive. Stop problems with bosses before they happen. After you've worked with him a while, you'll get to know what pushes your boss's buttons. Maybe he really hates late assignments or is an extreme stickler for details. Whatever the trigger, consciously adjust your work habits so that you don't pull it.

23. Bad bosses can turn what should be a dream job into an unholy nightmare. If you have exhausted all avenues of relief, including mediation and looking into a transfer to a different division, and if you're finding it increasingly hard to go to work in the morning because you know you'll have to deal with this person, it's time to think about getting a new job. Just as it is not unusual to leave a marriage because of the partners' incompatibility, it is hardly unheard of to leave a job because of an impossible boss. Just make certain that, before you abandon ship, you exhaust all the other options. Resist the temptation to exit at the first sign of friction.

COLLEAGUES

FROM

PURGATORY

24. Mark Twain once said that you can pick your friends, but you can't pick your relatives. It's similar in a work situation. You can choose your job, but you can't usually do much about choosing your colleagues. You play the hand you're dealt. And when you and your colleagues all have a competitive shot at advancement, the politics can get ugly. Envious colleagues are among the worst. Their envy often results from low self esteem. They expend enormous amounts of energy putting you down in an effort to make themselves look good. Don't play this game. Always act in a civil manner and go out of your way to acknowledge their strengths and encourage their own career development. You gain nothing by making an enemy. By making an effort instead to raise your coworker's self-esteem, you may succeed in shutting down the main engine of envy.

25. Your job depends on your coworkers. True, you owe your paycheck most directly to the boss, but, nowadays, as more companies structure work into team endeavors, it has become increasingly critical for you to operate well with a variety of people. Do what you can to emphasize collaboration over competition. Make no mistake, "friendly" competition can encourage peak performance, but competition becomes distinctly unfriendly when the *common* goals become obscured. Your real opponents are the other firms out in the world vying for *your* firm's business. If you and your colleagues think of one another as enemies, your team will fall apart. The most effective way to put an end to unhealthy rivalry is to be upfront with the rivals, giving them credit where credit is due, and pointing out the value of working together for *common* goals: "You and I both know it's better for both our careers if we just cooperate on this thing."

26. Colleagues may try to make you grist for their rumor mill. Collaborate in such an enterprise, and you could soon be ground to dust. Spreading rumors is unprofessional and will never reflect well on you. Manipulative colleagues who try to ensnare you into rumor mongering will have no problem blaming you when the day of reckoning arrives. Avoid this trap by either steering them off the subject, or by coming out and saying: "I really don't think this is an appropriate topic . . ." Or: "I don't want to deal in rumors." They'll take the hint—and may even admire you for having chosen what even they recognize as the high road.

27. If you're stuck with a colleague who doesn't understand the need to get assignments in on time, don't begin by lecturing your fellow worker, but start instead with better planning. Address issues rather than personalities. Set realistic deadlines and crystal-clear benchmarks to make sure the work is done. If necessary, sit down and draw up a schedule that details exactly who does what and when it's due. Having a clear plan makes it less likely that even the slow poke will lag behind. Once it's in black and white, there's no weaseling out.

28. Maybe you recall from a hazy Western Civ elective that Niccoló Machiavelli was a political theorist from renaissance Italy who wrote about how to get and keep power by becoming indifferent to moral considerations. Unfortunately, these days, "Machiavellian" colleagues are not hard to come by. However, the odds are that if you're being victimized by one, you're not alone in your organization. Unite with others to hold the Machiavellian offender accountable for her actions. Don't let her go unchallenged. Precisely because an appeal to fairness and conscience won't be of much use in changing her behavior, maintain careful records of what the offender does, when, and to whom. If you must appeal to higher authority to curb this individual, you will need a complete set of facts. Indeed, this file may become necessary for your own survival and for the survival of colleagues worth caring about.

29. If you and a colleague are actively competing for the same job, the situation can get uncomfortable and even downright nasty. It is always best to behave in a civil manner, even if the other person doesn't. Never stoop to his level. Do what you can to redirect focus from egos to issues: "Hey, Henry, I know we're going for the same job. You want it as much as I do. But I just want to let you know that whoever is picked, this is nothing personal. It's just a business decision. I have no intention of being an enemy." Don't delude yourself into thinking that the two of you will become best buddies, but it is better for both of you if you learn how to get along as colleagues. Today's rival may be tomorrow's boss— or a key subordinate on whom your continued authority and advancement depend.

30. Don't let disputes and rivalries get personal. Avoid criticizing colleagues on a personal level. Personal affronts escalate a bad situation into something worse. Never put it this way: "You're always like this. You're an impossible person to deal with." Better to say: "Bob, I have to be honest. I have a problem with the way you've been handling the Johnson account. Let me be specific . . . " Separate the person from the problem. Then attack the problem rather than the person.

31. You know the type. You're sitting in a meeting. You've just made a presentation, and a colleague chimes in: "That's nothing. Our division was able to turn a project like this around in under two weeks." One-uppers like this can be extremely annoying. Fortunately, most people recognize them for what they are— attention cravers. This being the case, the best way to deal with such folks is to give them what they want and then move on: "Yes, that's terrific, Sue—a real accomplishment. But let's get back to the present issue . . . " If the one-upper persists, she does so at her peril. For the conversation has moved on, and she'll look foolish.

32. Dealing with a tight-lipped colleague can be very difficult. What is he thinking? Where is he coming from? Such a person may be more dangerous than colleagues who telegraph their emotions all the time. Your best option is to try gradually to win a degree of trust, which may open the enigma up. Ask his opinion on several less-than-critical matters. Try to get him involved in some of your decision making.

33. If you feel that relations between you and a coworker have deteriorated beyond your ability to cope, call for intercession. Nothing punitive here, but an effort at mediating peaceful coexistence. If you have an understanding boss, you may want to have her meet with the two of you to try to settle the matter. Or you may want to consider preempting the situation by suggesting that the colleague would be happier in another division or department. Don't turn this into a showdown ("This town ain't big enough for the two of us!"), but make the prospect of a move appealing to the colleague's self-interest.

EMPLOYEES FROM HUNGER

34. Ah, you finally have the upper hand. You're the boss. The "problem person" is the employee. Yeah. Right. The fact is that difficult employees and subordinates can be among the most severely trying management challenges. It is not always easy to get maximum productivity out of your people and maintain a satisfied, loyal workforce. But it is these twin goals that lie at the heart of management.

35. "You just don't understand," a disgruntled subordinate wails. And you are convinced of his sincerity. You really *don't* understand. Now, what to do about it? Much—maybe most—workplace strife can be traced to basic misunderstanding. An employee who does not hand in work on time may not understand your deadlines. An employee who makes the same mistakes over and over may not completely understand what you expect. Communicate goals, rules, procedures, and expectations repeatedly and precisely. If necessary, meet with employees before the start of each project to explain in detail what you want done and when you want it done. Be aware that what seems obvious to you may not be evident to others.

36. Then there are those employees who take a leaf from Frank Sinatra's book and insist on doing things "their way." Initiative and independence can be valuable assets in a subordinate—up to a point. Swallow your ego a moment and consider that it is even possible that a subordinate may have a thing or two to teach *you*. However, if an independent streak is negatively affecting productivity, it's time for a little education. Explain to the employee—in private—that you and your company have rules, that you support and enforce the rules, and that you expect everyone to be a team player. If you want to maintain a critical degree of independence, end the conversation by encouraging the employee to come to you with suggestions and ideas, but, as far as actions go, he must adhere to established procedure.

37. Problems with particularly difficult employees should always be documented. If the moment arises when you need to discipline or dismiss this individual, you will have to marshal all the evidence you have to make your case. Such a record is also crucial in the event that a former employee brings suit for wrongful dismissal. Do not publicize your records, and if your company has a policy on personnel record keeping, adhere to it strictly. If it does not have such a policy, better formulate one—in consultation with qualified legal counsel.

38. Clockwatchers who spend their time in eager anticipation of 5 p.m. may actually be looking for a challenge. Maybe the work you have given them is not stimulating enough, so, instead of efficiently tackling the routine tasks assigned, they literally mark time. The best course of action in this case is to check in on their work periodically and, if it is at all possible, offer something more: "If you'd like some variety, Henry, I really could use someone to help me with . . ." If the employee doesn't respond to the challenge, chances are another motivational problem is at the root of his compromised productivity.

39. *Watch your back!* You've probably heard this phrase so often that it has by now receded meaninglessly into the background. Better bring it up to the front of your mind, because backstabbers are the worst. To your face, they sing your praises, but when you're out of earshot, they begin whittling away at your character. Whittling? Sometimes it's more like an H-bomb. Backstabbers must be stopped—fast. Keep your antenna out for trouble, and when you find it, meet with the backstabber in private. Let her know what you've heard: "You are certainly entitled to your personal opinions are about me, but I am reminding you that we are running a business here. If you have a legitimate business concern, I encourage you to bring it up with me directly. *Directly.* My door is open. What I will not tolerate are offensive comments behind my back." Confronting a backstabber requires courage as well as self-control. But if you are not firm now, the situation will only deteriorate.

40. *Why did I hire this guy? What was I thinking of?* If one of your recent hires appears to be drowning—and pulling you and your department down with him—you need to analyze the problem quickly. He could be underqualified, he could be qualified but doesn't feel sufficiently challenged to engage his full commitment, or he could be hiding deeper problems, ranging from emotional difficulties, financial afflictions, substance abuse—you name it. Meet early with an employee whose work is not up to par. Don't make threats, but offer whatever help you can afford to give without compromising present productivity. Offer, too, the means of measuring progress. Establish improvement goals as well as a timetable for realizing them. Check in frequently, and adhere to the schedule. If the employee fails to measure up according to the objective scales you have established, consider assigning less demanding work or terminating the employee.

41. One of the best ways to improve the productivity of difficult employees is with the classic carrot-and-stick method. We all crave recognition and reward. Define performance levels that warrant these, and issue such carrots when the employee attains the goals you've set. When the employee falls short of the mark, reiterate the guidelines and, if necessary, modify your measure of expectations. But hold the person to whatever you define. The "stick" you *actually* apply may be nothing more than a discussion of goals. The *implied* stick, of course, is the possibility of dismissal. Whatever you do, avoid bending the rules you set. Showing favorites is the surest way to create resentment among your team.

42. If an employee's performance or behavior has deteriorated beyond your capacity to resolve the situation, make use of your human resources department or, if you don't have such a department, call on some other in-house mediator. Enlarging the arena of the conflict may demonstrate to the employee that you don't regard this as a personal problem between the two of you. It is a business issue, an organizational issue, a corporate issue. HR can set up a meeting in which the employee's behavior and performance is discussed with you and with her. Remedies can be formulated, agreed on, recorded, and monitored. "Progressive discipline"—the human resources term for an orderly escalation of disciplinary steps that may eventuate in termination—can be instituted effectively and in a way that minimizes the company's legal exposure.

CLIENTS FROM

NEW YORK

43. "You call this a presentation? I call it #@$%*!" You just sit, phone receiver held two inches from your ear, and absorb the blows as they land. As usual, this client's not happy. Clients can be a lot like bosses, in that they control much more of your destiny than you may like to admit. The best thing you can do is try to understand your client from the beginning. Don't start out the relationship so busy to sell yourself that you fail to listen to him. One of the least understood aspects of communication is listening. If you are involved in the negotiations to bring the client on board in the first place, take notes, not just about what the client *says* he wants, but about what you *think* makes him tick. Create a picture of his expectations, of what motivates him, what turns him off, and so on. If you *haven't* been listening to this client, start now. And start listening from the beginning with your *next* client.

44. Set up lines of communications with your clients. Make sure they know exactly who to contact when a question or a problem arises. It's bad enough when a client experiences a problem. It's a disaster when the problem occurs, and she has no one to talk to about it. If you feel it's appropriate, offer to send regular status updates by letter, fax, e-mail, or some other means. Report on what you've done over the past week, month, quarter, or whatever time frame works best. Clients want to know how their money is being spent, and they want to assess the value you're providing. Frequent communication is equated with great service.

45. Is your client a screamer? Your first goal is to turn down the volume so that you can actually hear the problem. Allow a moment or two for venting, but resist the temptation to take the diatribe personally or to jump right in with a defense. Remember, your client may be so angry that he'd really like nothing more than for you to take it all *very* personally. However, you gain nothing by snapping at this bait. Avoid telling the screamer to "calm down." Instead, address him by name: "John, John—I hear that you're angry. But I need to understand what the problem is. I'm here. Take a breath and tell me. From the beginning." Hear the client out first before speaking. However, try interjecting a question or two that focuses on facts, not personalities, and that clarifies any points that remain unclear. You don't want to appear *totally* unresponsive. After you have the story, summarize your understanding of it. Then offer to work together on a solution: "John, I understand. Now, here are the three areas I suggest we work together on to get this back on track . . . " If you cannot come up with an instant analysis, let alone a solution, ask for time: "John, I'm going to need a day or two to work on a solution." However, you might find that simply giving the client an opportunity to vent will be sufficient to defuse the anger.

46. Here's a technique for working with inattentive clients who say one thing but then claim to have meant something entirely different. Play back their words to them: "Good. Now let me see if I understood you correctly. Bear with me a second. You are asking us to create a document that has the following elements . . . " This will prompt the client to confirm what she's just said. Not only will you ensure your understanding of the client's wishes and perspective, she will be put in a position to acknowledge that you've gotten the message loud and clear, thereby making a later denial less likely.

47. A classic technique to apply to really demanding clients is to undersell but overperform. "Yes, I think we can do that for you. It's going to be a little difficult because of thus and so, but we will give it our best." By lowering expectations just a notch, what you do deliver will seem that much more satisfactory. The worst thing to do is overpromise and underdeliver. Even if you perform well, you will have created a context of expectation that may lead to disappointment.

48. If you and a client are experiencing a particularly vexing problem, propose a face-to-face meeting. You need to establish human contact, and you need to see the gestures of body language that cannot be picked up over the phone. If at all possible, patch things up in person. It is your chance to tell him that he is important enough to warrant the effort, time, and expense of a special trip.

49. Many client-related problems can be prevented by developing effective contracts and agreements. A good contract clearly spells out expectations. It does not have to be a daunting document the size of the Treaty of Versailles, but it should unambiguously lay out who is responsible for what, when, and for how much. Don't leave important understandings to debatable, fallible memory. Define responsibilities and expectations, and commit them to paper at the outset of your relationship with a new client.

50. Gauge how much hand-holding difficult clients need, and plan your time accordingly. If you notice that the client runs her shop with an iron fist, odds are she will demand the same from you. Designate someone on your staff to act as the liaison or "point-person" for that client. This individual will be responsible for keeping the flow of information going in both directions and may be in almost daily contact with the client.

51. It's their money. True, you provide the value, but they spend the money. Before it ever becomes an issue, make sure your accounting and invoicing procedures and practices are clear, accurate, and easy to understand. No client likes to see the largest sum due next to such nebulous categories as "Miscellaneous." Such poor reporting invites distrust, an angry exchange, and delayed payment. Give a detailed accounting of your time and expenses, and be sure you can back it all up.

52. At some point, you may find yourself unable to serve a client effectively. If you and your client prove truly incompatible, it's not worth doing handsprings to retain the client. But you shouldn't burn any bridges, either. Take the high road: "I think you might be better served by going with another agency. If you'd like, I could suggest some agencies that might be able to help you more effectively than we can." No one likes to lose a client, but sometimes the fit is so bad that you're both better off parting ways. When that time comes, never relinquish self-control, always stay professional, and part on a positive, generous note.

SILENCING

A SCREAMER

53. They lose it. They just lose it. Whether it's a boss, an employee, client, coworker, subordinate—these are the people who can't avoid making a spectacle of themselves. When screamed at, the main thing to do is *don't scream back.* If you don't think you can resist the impulse, take a breath and remove yourself from the scene: "Let's talk—when we *can* talk."

54. The most important thing to remember about a screamer is that he demands attention and is willing to resort to juvenile means to get it. Well, then, pay attention—not to the screaming or the screamer, but to the root of whatever it is that's bothering him. Do your best to weather the storm of high-volume verbiage coming your way. Then step in with: "Hal, can we explore what's really the matter here? I need to understand . . ." Before speaking, wait for a lull. In the meantime, resist the impulse to respond to each accusation hurled at you.

55. Sometimes the best way to silence a screamer is to respond in a voice slightly softer than your normal speaking voice. This forces the other person to concentrate on listening to what you have to say. It also brings the decibel level down and makes it less likely that the other person will maintain her *fortissimo* volume.

56. Your responses should not mirror his. Remain calm and steady. "I hear what you are saying, but I'm not going to continue this way if you choose to shout. We are two adults who can solve our problems like adults. I'm ready to talk about solutions when you are." Such words may sound like they could come only from saints, but they will have to be *your* words if you want to get through to a screamer.

57. Never hang up on a screamer. This only gives her more ammunition to use against you later. If you want the offender to get off the line, try a calm response like: "I have to go right now. I will call you back in a few minutes." This gives both of you a cooling-off period and denies the other person what her rage craves: an immature response to stoke the fires of her anger.

58. If the screamer is a subordinate, try to move him to the privacy of your office. Here, calmly and coolly explain that this type of behavior is not tolerated and that there are other, more effective ways of expressing grievances. Do not embarrass the screamer any further in front of others, but do make it clear to subordinates that there are very real consequences to this type of behavior.

59. When and where appropriate, subordinates should be asked to apologize later for egregious public outbursts. No one likes to be subjected to these displays, and the offending party should be asked to show some contrition for unacceptable behavior. In your office, after you have calmly discussed the underlying grievance, say to the offender: "Now, Sarah, why don't you sit here a moment and collect yourself. Then, I think you'll feel better if you see Peter, Harry, Claire, and Frank and apologize to them for this loss of temper. I *think* you'll feel better, and I *know* they will feel better. You owe it to them."

60. It should not come as news that screaming bosses are more difficult to deal with than screaming subordinates. The boss holds more of the high cards. For that reason, it is even more crucial that you refrain from responding in kind. The best strategy is to ride out the storm and hope the realization dawns on him that this type of behavior will not yield the results he wants. After the energy of the rage is spent, ask for a meeting to discuss whatever *issue* has triggered the outburst: "Mr. Gregory, I appreciate your feelings, and, obviously, I want to resolve this situation. Can we sit down in a half hour so that you can tell me exactly what your expectations are?"

61. Often, you are not the intended target of rage. You've just been unlucky enough to wander into the line of fire. Or perhaps you present a handy "target of opportunity." But the real object of the screamer's anger lies elsewhere. And it may have absolutely nothing to do with work. While your role as a business person is not to be everyone's psychiatrist, you might nevertheless find it a necessary and compassionate act to lend a sympathetic ear. Working within your company's guidelines—and guided, too, by your own instincts and inclinations—you may want discreetly to suggest professional counseling. "It sounds like you've got some painful issues to deal with, John. I know you don't want them to interfere with your work. Maybe it's time to get some professional advice?"

RIPOSTING

RUDENESS

62. *Do unto others as you would have them do unto you.* If there ever was a time to practice the Golden Rule, it's when you deal with rude people. They'll interrupt you, they'll barge in, ignore you, needle you, and tick you off. Although the temptation is great, don't return such behavior in kind. The very best response to really rude behavior is to excuse yourself politely from the scene and offer to come back at a later time. This defuses tensions and communicates to the boor that you have no intention of exposing yourself to abuse. Yet it leaves open the door to communication and resolution.

63. *The filibuster:* the rambling verbiage of another that keeps you from speaking your piece. The most effective way to convert a monologue into a conversation is to break in with specific questions. Ask the offender: "Yes, Frank, but does that have any impact on the budget we're discussing right now?" The more specific the question, the more sharply focused on the subject at hand, the more likely the offender, as well as anyone else present, will realize that time is being wasted and that the moment for getting back on track is *now*.

64. "That was a good presentation, Bob. Glad to see things are starting to look up for you." Back-handed compliments can be particularly biting—and particularly undermining. As always, avoid responding in kind. Remain above the fray. Go over to the offender in private and say something like, "Thanks, Bill. I worked hard on it. But I'm not sure I understand what you mean by 'looking up.' Things are—and have been—just fine with me. Is there something we need to discuss?" Bill may deny that he meant anything by the comment. Or he may tell you that you're overreacting. Reply: "Well, I'm glad to hear it, because if there's something I've done to bother you, I'd like to correct it as soon as possible."

65. Some people, it seems, live to put others down. By diminishing you, they feel they are elevating themselves. Your sovereign defense against such an insecure individual is to recognize that it takes two to make her equation work. If you play along with her game and let a condescending remark wound you, you've handed the offender a victory. You know your self worth. Don't let anyone else define it for you. Learn to tune out the negative comments and, instead, focus your energy on accomplishing tasks that will help you shine all the more brilliantly.

66. Office snoops forever ferret out information they think they can use to gain power. They pepper you with annoying questions and won't leave you alone until their curiosity is satisfied. But, remember, you're not on the witness stand, and you don't even have to engage snoops in conversation: "I think it's best if we dropped the subject." Or just switch the topic altogether. That's a very effective way to get the snoop to lose interest in speaking to you. Pretty soon, even the most determined snoop will conclude that you're not much use as a source of information and will leave you alone.

67. Don't tolerate talk behind people's back. Gossip and innuendo destroy trust and, therefore, undermine your team: "Have you heard that Janet in sales . . ." Quickly steer the conversation onto a different topic, or confront the issue of gossip straight on: "Look, I really am not interested in talking about that. If I want to know more about Janet, I can always ask her in person. I'm not sure she'd like the fact that you're talking about her this way." Zap!

68. One of the best ways to riposte rudeness is to set an example of courtesy. If you are in management, setting the tone of politeness to others in the office will yield long-term benefits. No one ever died fom saying "please," "thank you," or "you're welcome." And, more to the point, no one's authority was ever undermined by such words. Courteous office behavior helps make business interaction more pleasant and more efficient. The good feelings are projected to your customers and clients as well. And that means more business.

69. If the rude person in your office is a subordinate, you have leverage. Use it wisely. Meet with him in private: "It's come to my attention that you have said a number of things your colleagues have found offensive. It's not my intent to name names, but several people have told me the same story . . ." It's important to present the facts, but not to corner the offender. Give him a chance to respond and to explain. Superficial rudeness may be a sign of more deeply seated frustrations. Indeed, the rude behavior may have been this employee's unconscious way of getting you to talk to him. Be receptive to the issues. At the very least, give the subordinate an opportunity to vent.

70. Look in the mirror. Sometimes the rude behavior of others may be a response to signals you may not even be aware you're sending. Examine how you deal with others. Do you let them finish sentences? Do you thank them for a job well done? Do you ask them politely to do certain tasks? Ask a friend—one who won't betray your confidence—for an honest assessment. The personality of a group is largely derived from the perceived personality of its leader. Are you behaving as you want others to behave?

71. Deflate rudeness by demonstrating that it has no effect on you. Smile. If a doubtful remark comes your way, smile. Then quietly monitor the situation.

OUTMANEUVERING SCHEMERS

72. Schemers prefer plotting to playing by the rules. They'd rather weave plots than work honestly to achieve their goals. Do not attach yourself to such people. They will get you nowhere fast. Send strong signals that you will not be joining in any conspiratorial schemes. Leave under-the-table politics to someone else. Most shortcuts are dead ends. The high road means doing your work and doing it well.

73. Learn to recognize warning signs. Sometimes the schemer is obvious. She telegraphs her intentions with every move, and it becomes obvious that you've been chosen as a target. Other times, the schemer may wear sheep's clothing and even pretend to be your friend. Unfortunately, most people learn only from experience, and, once you've been "schemed," it may be too late for anything but damage control. Learn from experience.

74. If you believe that someone is secretly working against you in the office, make an effort to document everything suspicious. When the moment is right, you will want to be able to make your case to those above you calmly, rationally, and with all the evidence in hand. Don't make it personal. Bring to the table whatever facts you have: "Boss, I recently learned that a 'private memo' has been circulating saying that I made several mistakes on the Jones account. I obtained a copy of the memo, and I wanted to go over it point by point before people started believing the nonsense it contains."

75. Confronting a schemer can be dangerous, but sometimes it must be done. "You know, John, we don't have to be friends, but I don't think we have to be enemies, either. If you have a problem with something I've done, I am eager to talk about it with you and try to resolve the problem. But I'm not happy hearing about what you say behind my back. I don't do it to you . . . "

76. Be ready to call in some chits. Taking your case to higher-ups in order to acquire allies may be risky, but sometimes necessary. If the person scheming against you is angling for the same promotion you've targeted, for example, you will always want those in a position of power to know that you handle yourself professionally and tactfully. Keep the lines of communication open with these people, but always keep the conversation on a professional plane. Don't resort to personal attacks.

77. Try to work closely with the schemer. There's a saying that goes, "The only thing I keep closer than my friends are my enemies." There's a kernel of truth there. Without revealing that you know they're scheming, try to win them over to your side. You may know at the outset that you probably won't succeed, but you will also send the signal that you are "on to them" and won't be taken by surprise.

78. Sometimes the opposite tack works better. Schemers will try to set you up for a fall. Try not to have to rely on the potential schemer. He will try to find a way to trap you into looking bad. By making sure that you've covered all your bases and by lessening your dependence on the schemer, you deny him the means to make you look bad.

79. Ask for clarification. If a schemer seems to be asking for an inordinate amount of information from you, tell him that you're busy and ask for his request in writing: "Sorry, Bill, I'm pushing on this project right now. Can you send me a memo or an e-mail on whatever you need?" If the request comes through, you'll have physical evidence of the scheming. Of course, your asking for the request in writing might just be enough to stop him in his tracks.

80. Schemers almost inevitably try to win over allies to their cause. It is very important to keep tabs on what alliances are being formed without appearing too nosy. Your objective is to hold on to your present allies, write off current enemies, and win over neutral parties. And do it all with tact and diplomacy—something the schemer will likely not possess.

81. Play your game for the long run. Schemers are usually good at winning tactical battles, but often lose the war. While scheming may help them to temporarily, those in authority usually come to recognize their dangerous patterns of behavior, and they begin to wonder when the schemes will be used against *them*. Your goal is to keep to your strategic objectives over the long term and not become obsessed with winning or losing a battle or two.

NAVIGATING THE EGOTIST'S WORLD

82. Me, me, me, I, I, I . . . It's not the sound of an opera singer warming up. It's an egotist singing the only notes he knows. Working with people like this can be difficult because they really can't see beyond themselves—and egocentric bosses can be among the most difficult, because they're in a position of power. They can *act* on their egotism. It is well to remember that self-centered bosses are usually quite worried about how they appear to those above them. It's important that you help—or appear to help—the boss boost his own image, especially when it comes to his or her superiors. Maybe then the boss will *see* you.

83. You don't *have* to take credit all the time, especially where the boss is concerned. If she's an egotist, try this next time you come up with a great idea. Phrase it in such a way that she will credit herself as the source of your inspiration: "I was thinking about what you said at the last staff meeting, and, you know, you're right. There *are* ways we can cut costs. Here's what I was thinking we could do—based on your idea, of course . . ." Transparent flattery? You bet. Think your boss will see through it? Fat chance.

84. An egotistical boss who likes to show off is hard to one-up. Don't even try. The most effective strategy is not to let him faze you. Ultimately, you've got to believe that your value to the company will be based on performance. And you can't afford to believe that you'll change your boss's behavior. So the best you can do is work to earn your boss' confidence and just sit back with everyone else and watch the egotistical display. In time, it is likely that other people who matter will see the egotist for who he really is.

85. You've met her—the egotistical colleague who is always right, always perfect, and always full of...herself. Deflate this individual s-l-o-w-l-y. Listen to her tall tale, then gently press for details. "That's great, Gail. Tell me, exactly how many orders did you fill to reach that quota?" Don't be obnoxious about it. But do put her on notice that she can't continue to run roughshod over the facts without your being there to trip her up.

86. Avoid taunts and antagonism—especially if you and your egotistical friend are in front of the boss. Let's revisit Gail. Always be ready to give the great inflator a diplomatic way out: "Oh, of course, you probably were thinking of the quota for the previous quarter. Simple mistake." This gets her off the hook, but quietly asserts your power over her. It's a classic routine: "I know that you know that I know..."

87. "Well, I finally finished the project—just in time," you say to a colleague. To which he responds: "That's nothing. I got my assignment done in half the time!" This takes patience. Lots of it. Grit, then grin. A compulsion to put you down by invidious comparison is a bid for attention. Your best bet is to grant recognition when recognition's due, but also to tease—lightly and politely—when the colleague crosses the line: "I heard very good things about that last report you wrote. As far as the deadline goes, gee, Sally, we all know you're the fastest gun West of the fax machine . . ."

88. Then there are the colleagues who have answers for just about everything. They seem especially interested in making you look bad in front of others by demonstrating what they believe is their vast knowledge. Fight back not by trying to beat them at their own game, but with a gentle shove and a tender trip. Do your homework. When a particular subject comes up, speak with authority: "I don't think you have it quite right there, Ed. We sold that model last year and then discontinued the line. Check the catalogue." Caution: Don't attack the person. Instead, marshal the facts.

89. Egotistical subordinates can be a nightmare for any manager. Not only would they have you believe the company couldn't function without them, they'd probably take credit for the sun rising in the east, if they thought they could get away with it. They can be an especially bad influence when you're trying to build and maintain a team. You should never behave as if you are intimidated by them or give them the impression they have "it up on you." Maybe you really are intimidated. In that case, the curtain's up, and you had better give an award-winning performance—if you want to retain leadership.

90. Like the proverbial optimist who sees the water glass half full rather than half empty, you can also look at egotistical employees as team players—who haven't yet climbed on board. Tell them in private that their actions are keeping the entire group from achieving what's got to be done. Be specific. Cite an example or two. Sometimes group pressure works better than pressure from above. If necessary, peers can be brought in to put pressure on the offending individual.

91. Egotists huff, puff, and strut. Just remember that they are close to starvation. Deny them the attention they crave, and they begin to shrivel. Because they lack inner strength, they need to borrow your strength in the form of praise and admiration. This puts you in a very powerful position. Grant the egotist what he wants—albeit sparingly and on your own terms.

CARE
AND FEEDING
OF PASSIVE-
AGGRESSIVE
PEOPLE

92. Passive-Aggressive people seem meek, complacent, and easy-going, but have a knack for sabotage. You ask for some critical task to be performed, and, somehow, it remains undone. "Oh, I'll get to it. Don't worry." But you *should* worry. The first rule for dealing with passive-aggressives is to monitor them, keep them on schedule, check their progress, give repeated instructions, and set objectives and goals. In short, respond to passivity with an active determination to keep the passive-aggressive on track.

93. Don't try to deal with the underlying sources of the passive-aggressive personality. You have neither the time nor the expertise to practice psychiatry. Instead, address behavior and the products of behavior by the steady application of schedules, evaluation of progress, and repetition of instructions, goals, and objectives. Get what you need—then move on.

94. Passive-aggressive behavior often takes the form of condescending remarks directed at you. A passive-aggressive boss won't put you down *too* directly, but may well say something like, "This is a straightforward project. You can handle it." Respond by recognizing that your boss is tactless, and that tactless people can't help but say hurtful things. Choose to concentrate on how skilled, efficient, and effective you are. Do a great job. Let the boss deal with his own inadequacies and lack of communication skill.

95. The next time you experience passive-aggressive condescension, blow right by it with a demonstration of utter competence. *Boss:* "Sarah, I don't suppose you were able to finish the Young account . . ." *Sarah:* "I completed it last night and have moved on to Grierson. I need to talk to you about the fact that Grierson is sixty days in arrears . . ."

96. Fight condescension by behaving and performing in ways that earn the respect and admiration of your colleagues and subordinates. Sooner or later, your boss will pick up on the signals from everyone else and start treating you with greater respect.

97. The term *passive-aggressive* says a lot about the essence of this difficult person's personality. She is fundamentally dishonest—not only with others, but with herself. A typical passive-aggressive mode is hypocrisy, double-dealing, in which you are misled or misrepresented. Often, the hypocrite will solicit your opinion or aid, or will get you to confide in her, only to stab you in the back later. The best defense against this is a proactive one: ask direct questions that require direct answers. Try to hang on to facts. Furthermore, when you recognize that you are working with a hypocrite, refuse to accept anything she says at face value. Investigate and confirm. Proceed slowly. Use confirming memos before taking action on projects, and be sure that you get the hypocrite to sign off on them.

98. Probably no one is all bad or all good—completely hypocritical or completely honest. If you find yourself in a situation where you feel you have been misled or even betrayed, salvage what you can by looking for areas of compromise and agreement. Since you have to keep working with this difficult person, a compromise route is better than a showdown. *You:* "I thought we had agreed on A, B, and C across the board. That was something we had talked about and confirmed." *Hypocrite:* "No, I never said that..." *You:* "Can we at least agree on A and B? The evidence for these seems overwhelming to me..."

99. Confronted with a passive-aggressive deception, be deceptive yourself. Your supervisor has given you vague directions concerning a project. No wonder! The project looks doomed, and, obviously, your passive-aggressive supervisor is setting you up to take the fall when the thing collapses. There's no productive way you can actually accuse him of this strategy, however. Instead of directing your response at him, therefore, direct it at the system and paint a temporary us-against-them scenario: "I don't know what Corporate can be thinking, giving us this project. It's going to give our department a black eye, if we don't think of some alternatives. Can we discuss a few ideas . . ."

100. A favorite passive-aggressive ploy is to bury you in details. Pile on enough of these—the more irrelevant the better—and a colleague or supervisor is sure to kill any project you come up with. And it will all be done under the guise of "just doing her job." If you can't work around this kind of passive-aggressive resistance by appealing to other authorities and presenting them with evidence in support of your project, try compromising by scaling back what you're asking for: "Well, why don't we agree on a probationary period? Let's set a cost and time limit, and let's set some performance parameters. If we don't make the numbers, we redesign the project."

101. Don't make the mistake of rejecting all criticism as the work of a passive-aggressive personality. Your supervisors, coworkers, subordinates, and customers do have legitimate concerns, and you can't always think of everything. Evaluate criticism. Accept it gratefully and graciously as a gift. If, however, you are convinced that you are being smothered in a wet blanket, resist by doing the best job you possibly can; by accumulating objective evidence and facts in support of what you propose; by garnering support wherever you can find it; and by remaining obviously optimistic in the tone and content of what you say. Finally—and this can be the hardest part—be willing to compromise and modify your idea.

LAZY
NO MORE

102. There are many ways *not* to do work, but the simplest way not to do it is . . . *not to do it.* Faced with a subordinate who watches the clock and puts forth no effort, you can rant, rave, and threaten termination, or you can take a more constructive approach. Begin by double-checking your own part of the work: Have you made the assignment clear, and have you given full and realistic instructions? If you are convinced that the problem does not lie with you, hold off accusing and berating the shirker. Instead, ask him what's wrong. Let him talk. Then really think about what he says. Perhaps he is revealing the keys that will unlock his motivation.

103. A subtle but significant alternative to asking questions is deliberately to put your criticism in the *form* of a question: "Patricia, why do you think you are having so much trouble finishing your assignments on time? Do you have any suggestions for getting your productivity up to an acceptable level?"

104. Is clockwatching an isolated phenomenon or a regular pattern at your shop? If it's become the rule rather than the exception, all the threats and criticism in the world aren't going to make your organization more productive. Instead, make some changes in the work environment. Introduce programs to build pride in performance, to increase camaraderie, to build a team. Create discussion groups or "quality circles," which will give subordinates an ownership stake in productivity. Do what you can to make the work more challenging and meaningful.

105. Is your performance being dragged down by a dawdling colleague? Working is, in part, a social event, and some people like to loiter, pass the time of day, arrive for meetings fashionably late, and waste time in interminable small talk. Instead of clamming up and then later blowing up at these maddeningly irritating people, lend a helping hand. Work with the dawdler to help him get organized and efficient. If you are teamed with one of these folks, spend time laying out procedures. Create detailed schedules that are loaded with tangible milestones to mark progress. Formulate a series of tasks and deadlines.

106. If a lazy colleague is habitually late, don't bother talking to her about the problem. Just start everything without her. If the meeting was called for 9 a.m., resist the temptation to turn in exasperation to the assembled throng with: "Well, Marjorie is late as ususal. We'd better wait." Instead, a simple "It's nine. Let's get started" is in order. When Marjorie finally does walk in, look up at her, but don't say a word. Try not even to break the cadence of the ongoing discussion. She'll get the message.

107. Some bosses have an uncanny talent for putting off decisions, stalling and procrastinating, perhaps in the hope that a problem or issue will simply go away. Don't be dragged down by them. Instead, help your boss over his inertia by doing whatever you can to make the decision easier. If there's legwork or research to do, do it. Impress him with your efficiency while greasing the tracks for him.

108. Be bold when you're dealing with procrastinators. This may mean devoting your energy to doing rather than waiting. Assume additional responsibility for doing what's not getting done. Take over tasks that are languishing. Just be careful that you don't overstep your own authority. Usually, procrastinating bosses and colleagues will be relieved that you've done the jobs they find onerous or daunting.

109. One sure way to avoid getting a job accomplished is to blow it out of all proportion. Your task is to shrink work down to an appropriate size. In working with a person who tends to magnify jobs assigned to her, emphasize priorities and deadlines. You might even employ a rudimentary rating scale: priority A, B, C. Agree on strict deadlines and enforce them. Remember, as a general rule, work expands to fill the time allotted to it. When you are dealing with a magnifier, the work expands far beyond the time allotted. Enforce deadlines rigorously.

110. Perhaps you were a picky eater when you were a child. If you had a wise and patient mom, she understood that the best thing to do was to avoid heaping adult-sized portions on your plate, and instead gave you a little bit at a time. Try this strategy with people who tend to magnify the scope of assignments. You don't have to give them less work, just break it down for them into a series of smaller tasks. Alternatively, suggest that *their* first step should be breaking the work down for themselves and assigning timelines for each phase. Just be certain that you discuss and approve all deadlines.

111. Then there are the genuinely, out-and-out, no-holds-barred lazybones who deal with work by trying to palm it off on you. They'll put the request in the form of an appeal for a favor. They'll devote the energy they should focus on getting the work done to cajoling and massaging you instead. Be strong. You don't need a reason to decline doing someone else's work. Say no, perhaps adding a *mild* expression of regret: "I'm sorry, Jake. I can't help you with this." If you find such refusals difficult, practice at home. Ask your spouse or even your kid to play the role of the imposer. Rehearse till you get it right.

BEATING UP
BULLIES

112. Sailing is not smooth under Captain Bligh. Set a goal not to get your boss to adore you (that's almost certainly unrealistic), but to get her to treat you in a civil and courteous manner. You have the right to expect this much. Don't pick a fight with a tyrant, don't be deliberately confrontational, but do prepare to act. Present a firm and strong presence—but one that is unemotional. Keep conducting business. If you are abused, respond in a manner that focuses on business. *Boss:* "You know, you'd better start working a lot harder than you do around here, and you'd better get on the ball. I don't want to see you back in my office until this assignment is done. Is that coming through loud and clear?" *You:* "I understand how important this account is, and I'll do what needs to be done. But there is no reason for you to put it the way you do. Trying to make me feel bad is not going to get the work done any better or faster."

113. Let the tyrant huff and puff. Just step around his wind. *Boss:* "You guys are absolutely pathetic. I'm away for two days, and the whole office goes to hell. Where is the Smith contract? Why isn't it complete and on my desk? Can't you do anything right?" *You:* "Three issues remain outstanding, which require discussion between you and Smith. Let me outline them for you, together with my suggestions . . ."

114. A bully is never a solo act. She requires a victim. Choose not to be a victim. Examine why you allow yourself to be intimidated. If it comes down to fear of losing your job, well, that's a very real fear and a legitimate concern. But is it any way to live? If you chronically fear losing your job—and if you shape your relationship to your boss according to this fear—consider a new job. Discreetly, quietly start looking. Begin the search before you become a total emotional wreck who will be useless to any employer.

115. In the workplace, the classic bully shuts her eyes and ears. Do what you can to pry them open. *Boss:* "I told you that I don't want to hear about overhead. If you can't do what you're assigned, just clear out of here. Do you understand me?" *You:* "I understand that you don't want me to figure in overhead, but, if I don't, the costs I give you won't mean much . . ." *Boss:* "Don't you ever give up? Are you starting with me . . ." *You:* "Pardon me, Mary, but I'm not through. I need half a minute to finish. Overhead accounts for 30 percent of costs in this case. Now, I think I can accomplish what you want by taking a different approach. Do you want to hear me out?"

116. The great American jurist Learned Hand once bewailed the absence of justice "in the streets and in the courts." Be aware that going over the head of a bully boss might backfire. Bullies are often born of bullies, and the chances are that your boss's approach merely reflects the attitude of senior management. Go to them, and your boss may come out looking like a hero. As to you—well . . . Just be advised that it's almost always best to resolve problems "within the family."

117. Don't counterattack the bully's attack. Instead, take it apart, piece by piece. Respond as if the diatribe were rational conversation: "Jack, I understand A, C, and D. I even agree with A and could be persuaded about C. But B totally confuses me. Can you clarify that for me?"

118. Maybe the bully would benefit from shock therapy. You might be surprised to know that such treatment is within your power. Your boss starts bellowing, calling you names, and opening up with the usual threats of termination. You can cower, which will ensure that your boss will continue to treat you this way. You can appeal to higher authority, which may work—or which may fail, producing possibly grave consequences for yourself. Or you can calmly issue a command: "Mr. Thomas, please sit down." That alone will put the bully off balance. Continue: "I understand that you are upset. But that gives you no right to talk to me like that. I am due common courtesy and human respect. That's the way I wish to be treated. Now, if you can speak to me in a civil manner, I'll remain in this office, and we can work out the production problem together."

119. Bullies are usually pretty narrow people. While their behavior is most unpleasant, you can at least predict it. You can count on being treated rudely, and you can prepare accordingly. More difficult to cope with is the explosive personality, whose anger erupts unexpectedly. You press the wrong button, and—kaboom! If you can avoid sensitive issues, do so. But when the explosion comes, figure out a way to endure the blast. You can simply exercise patience. Don't try to calm the man down. Just wait for him to run out of steam. You don't have to remain completely silent. Try repeating his name: "Fred, Fred, listen a moment. Fred . . ." If the display is really fierce, remove yourself—fast: "Fred, I'll talk to you later." And you're out the door.

120. Reward and reinforce calm and civil discourse. Fred blows up, rants, raves—then calms down and starts speaking rationally. Don't pick this moment to act on your own anger and irritation by hollering back or refusing to listen. Acknowledge and reinforce Fred's new-found (and doubtless fragile) rationality by hearing him out. Try to engage him. Make liberal use of the pronoun *we*, and demonstrate that you're on his side: "Fred, I understand how critical this project is. But we can pull it off—if we don't let ourselves fall apart. Let's keep the team strong and work on a solution we'll all be pleased with."

121. Another form of bullying is intimidation. The language may not be overtly abusive, but it is nevertheless intended to make you feel inferior. Let's say you propose an approach to a certain project. Instead of commenting on—or even criticizing—the approach, the intimidating bully will say: "You've *got* to be kidding. No one would even *think* of doing it that way." Even if you are confident of your abilities, it's difficult to remain poised under such sweeping fire. But poised and calm is precisely the way you must act. Rehearse replies at home. Use a tape recorder, if you like, or enlist the aid of friends and family in role playing. You can't argue with an intimidator, since his remarks are not logical. They are assertions. Mere bully talk. However, if you remain calm, you can reply with facts rather than an argument: "This approach will accomplish such and such and will reduce costs by so much . . ." Don't even bother to deal with the intimidator's jabs at you. Counter punch with facts.

CRUSHING
CONSTANT
CRITICS

122. If everything we did were perfect, there would be no need for criticism. Since that won't ever be the case, we'll just have to accept the fact that someone will always be around to criticize our work. The issue is not whether you'll encounter criticism, but what kind and how much. People who can find nothing positive to say and dote on doling out negativity are hard to work for and with. But they're here, and you have to find a way of coping with them.

123. A critical boss who never offers any praise may be either sending you the signal that you're not up to the work, or, more likely, letting you know that he just can't manage people very well. Good managers always use a series of carrots as well as sticks to motivate their people. Sticks alone will not get you very far. With overly critical bosses, be ready to meet criticism with facts: "I understand what you're saying, but here are the notes from the last meeting. You wanted the report done by Wednesday and in the same format as the last one." Make no further comment.

124. Offer to sit down with the boss to work out a plan to prevent future mistakes. Taking a proactive stance is your best—and most effective—alternative. This doesn't guarantee that your boss will like it, especially if he misses getting all that ammunition he so desperately craves. But at least he cannot fault you for wanting to prevent a repeat performance. And maybe—just maybe—he'll rise to an appropriate level of maturity.

125. Be prepared to deal with colleagues who make it a habit to throw cold water on your every idea. If you anticipate this happening, go into meetings well prepared to counter every argument she may offer. Consider sending up a trial balloon by running your idea past the troublesome colleague before the meeting. At least you'll have some idea where you stand. It is also possible that, by consulting with this person, you will offer her an ownership stake in the idea and thereby head off, eliminate, or blunt the expected criticism.

126. Appealing first to less critical colleagues will help you build a coalition of support that may intimidate even the bitterest of critics. Once he realizes that his argument will be challenged by more than one person, he may tone down his rhetoric.

127. Ask for specifics. Offhanded remarks such as "It can never be done" should not go unchallenged: "Well, Bill, I'm interested in hearing your perspective. Can you detail exactly how it is that this plan will not work?" Your objective is to put the critic in his corner without actually picking a fight.

128. Don't get personal. The minute criticism gets personal, both critic and target lose. Don't respond to criticism with a personal counter-attack: "You're always like this. I wonder how your wife puts up with you." Sad to say, remarks like that get said more often than many are willing to admit. Despite the venom critics may hurl your way, resist the temptation to reply a with shot below the belt.

129. Critical colleagues may well be masking their own insecurities. Perhaps you two are competing for the same job—and the other person fears you have the edge. Perhaps the critic is just congenitally jealous. Before you succumb to criticism and let your self-confidence suffer, analyze motive and source. The cruel words may really have little to do with you or your ability.

130. What if the critic is a chronic *self*-critic? Some people put themselves down in the hope that others will come along and tell them how great they are. Yet, often, they don't believe your reassurances. If you are the boss, it's best to address—gently and considerately—the issues that may be causing anxiety. Just don't get into the habit of doling out praise indiscriminately. You have to assume that your employees—most of the time—behave as adults capable of dealing with both criticism and praise.

131. If you can't beat 'em, try joining 'em. If you meet with unrelenting criticism, try bringing the critic into your camp: "Sue, I know you have some strong opinions about this, and I thought it would be best, the next time I do this, if you and I went over the project in detail, so I could get your perspective early on." There is no better way to de-fang a critic than to make your work partly theirs.

PUNCTURING

PERFECTIONISTS

132. We all know what a nitpicker is. Someone who insists on absolute perfection in tasks of little importance. But did you ever think of where the word comes from? Literally, a nitpicker is somebody who searches through a person's hair or an animal's fur for nits—the minuscule larvae of lice! Next time you are confronted by a nitpicking boss or colleague, deflate her in your mind by thinking of the root of the word. That should help you put the nitpicker in perspective.

133. Nitpickers are usually hard workers with little self-esteem and, often, limited creativity. They don't trust others to do a good job, and, therefore, they have trouble delegating tasks. When they do delegate, they look over your shoulder and breathe down your neck, then focus on minute details that are of little consequence. You can cope with the nitpicker in two ways. First, double check your own work to make sure that it is as close to perfection as possible. This will tend to preempt the nitpicker and, perhaps, win his confidence—eventually. Second, try directing the nitpicker's attention to some more meaningful task or some more meaningful aspect of the task you're performing. Hint: Ask for assistance or advice concerning something truly important.

134. Perfectionists can be inflexible, closed off to any ideas but their own. Your best chance to get the perfectionist's ear is to appeal to her self-interest or, at least, to your mutual interest. Don't present "my" idea, but focus on how the idea meets objectives the perfectionist boss or colleague is always talking about. Then show how these objectives mesh with those of management and will lead to advancement for both of you.

135. Perfectionist subordinates can be difficult to deal with if they expect too much from themselves and fear that they can never live up to the ideal they have set. Such people polish and polish their work and are so reluctant to let it go that projects fall behind schedule or fail to get finished at all. Your task is to put them back in touch with reality. Explain that a given task has more than one dimension: Yes, the project must be done well, but excellent performance also requires keeping within budget and meeting deadlines. Of necessity, succeeding in these dimensions requires compromise. Without infinite funds and infinite time, perfection is impossible.

136. A practical way to help the perfectionist is to work with her on time-management techniques. Perfectionists thrive on a strong sense of accomplishment, but they are often so overwhelmed by their own standards that they accomplish little. Help the perfectionist manage time by showing her how to break up work into stages. The sense of having completed one stage may make moving on to the next stage easier.

137. The boss who demands perfection may be as out of touch with reality as the perfectionist subordinate or colleague. Do not respond to demands for perfection with protests that such quality is impossible to achieve or beyond your ability. Instead, talk about balancing priorities. "Boss, if we use that grade of material, we'll be 25 percent over budget. Is that okay?" Or: "Mr. Reynolds, machining the parts three times will require refiguring the schedule—adding at least a week—and revising the budget upward. I'd say we'll be over our target by 20 percent. How do you want me to proceed?"

138. For some, perfectionism takes a maddeningly unyielding turn. Such people insist on following instructions or "policy" to the letter, even in situations that call for a measure of creativity and spontaneity. If you confront an unyielding subordinate, she's likely to express frustration: "But, boss, you've told me always to follow your orders . . ." This may be true enough—and that makes the situation all the more frustrating. Instead of berating the employee for a lack of initiative or common sense, change the way you give instructions. When you know that a given project will require the exercise of judgment to meet unpredictable circumstances, define a range of acceptable actions instead of a single option. For example: "Bill, we'd like to pay no more than $25 per gross for widgets, but if it will mean getting them shipped before March, you can go as high as $27. If you have to split the order between March and April, that's fine, too. I trust your judgment. Use it."

139. Perfectionists sometimes defend themselves by adopting a know-it-all attitude, flaunting their intelligence and their competence. In a just world, the know-it-alls would be easy to deflate because they'd lack real substance. However, the irritating fact is that know-it-all perfectionists are often quite competent—even dazzling. That makes them all the more obnoxious and difficult to deal with. The best way of handling this kind of perfectionist is to milk him for all he's worth. Use his expertise. This does not mean relinquishing the floor to him at meetings or piling on the work. Instead, formulate probing questions, and keep him on his toes by checking and verifying what he says. Use him as the valuable resource he is.

140. A perfectionist boss can come on like a slave driver, insisting that you put in the extra hours and additional sweat required to meet unrealistically high standards. You have several options to ease the pressure. Probably the best option is to negotiate better terms. "Elaine, it is getting impossible to do this much work at the quality level we need to achieve. Can we talk about some ways to ease the burden?"

141. Another way of dealing with unrealistic demands is to delegate and divide them. See if the assignment can be broken up and parceled out to others. Enlist the aid of your colleagues and subordinates. As the old saying goes, many hands make light work.

OUTMANIPULATING

THE

MANIPULATIVE

142. In the world of work, everyone manipulates others now and then, applying pressure here and persuasion there. But manipulation gets out of hand when you are exploited, deceived, or otherwise abused. Your mother told you that two wrongs never make a right. Your first choice in dealing with a manipulator who crosses the line should be to do the right thing. Don't try to outmaneuver the manipulator. Instead, make an appeal to her sense of fairness. See if this moves things your way. For example: "Boss, I know that you are always concerned about being fair, so I don't think you realize the extent of the problem your decision has caused me . . ." Express your assumption that the manipulative treatment is an oversight that the other person will be anxious to correct.

143. You may be unfortunate enough to encounter a supervisor, colleague, or even a subordinate who attempts to manipulate you into a position of undeserved blame. It usually works like this: At some time, you are asked for an opinion on a project. You off-handedly mention that the project "looks good." Later, the project is put into operation, only to fall flat. Before you know it, it becomes known as *your* project. Don't absorb all the blame: "You're not suggesting that I was responsible for the project, are you?" This question alone may be sufficient to redirect blame more fairly. But what if the response is something like, "Well, who else threw their support behind it?" Launch into an explanation: "The project did look good to me, that's true. Obviously, it looked good to a lot of people, including the Steering Committee, which is most responsible for having generated it. Hindsight is always 20/20, so we should probably stop blaming and start rethinking our options."

144. Liars are the ultimate manipulators. They seek not only to manipulate people, but truth itself. It is very important that you steer clear of dealing with personalities or motives when confronting a liar. Go straight to the *facts*. Present the *facts*. Let the *facts* expose the liar and his lie. Don't be too eager to pass judgment yourself. Let others come down on the offender.

145. It is possible to lie—to state something as fact that is untrue. It is also possible to deceive by telling half-truths, selectively omitting certain facts. Avoid pouncing on the omission. Instead, plug the gap casually, without making a major issue of it. "Oh, Bill, that's right. But you didn't mention the cost of the part. At $35, it adds quite a cost burden." Avoid reference to motives, and don't pass judgments. Just be johnny-on-the-spot with the missing information. You'll make your point, and very powerfully.

146. Wheeler-dealers offer dubious quid pro quos: "If you do this for me, I'll do that for you." When it comes to dealing with colleagues and supervisors, you've got to assume that they are honest and straightforward—until they do something that convinces you otherwise. After a promise is broken, you'll probably continue to have to work with the manipulator, but at least you'll be on your guard. Make liberal use of confirming memos and memos of understanding. Don't rely on verbal promises. Don't do something because you are promised something else in return. Instead, act in a way that is consistent with doing a good job and that shows that you are reasonable, cooperative, and dependable.

147. Don't let yourself be flattered into doing something stupid. "You are so good at expressing yourself, I'd like you to write up my report for me. No one else could do it as well." Better think past the kind words: Do you really want to write a report someone else will get credit for? Acknowledge the compliment, then move on: "Sid, I appreciate your confidence in me. But no one can match the conviction and depth of the person who is *really* responsible for the report. I'll be happy, though, to look at your draft when you finish it—if you still want my help."

148. Holding the bag—not a comfortable assignment. You support an idea, and you get a colleague to second your enthusiasm. The project suddenly goes south. The finger points at you, and now your "friend" denies having ever supported the proposal at all: "I never said I thought it would work." When this happens, it's really too late to do much but trade accusations and dirty stares. The more effective defense is proactive. Be sure that the support you gather is solid: "Jim, I appreciate your support for the project. I am going to feature your name *prominently* in my proposal memo. I'll copy you on it, of course."

149. Con artists don't just work the streets. They're in the office, too. Slick operators like to bend the rules, and get you to help them do it. Pretty soon, you find yourself more or less entangled in somebody else's schemes. You don't have to walk away from an office con artist. You *can* offer help—but help that is strictly according to the rules. You can also respond to his request for a favor by asking a lot of questions. The con artist wants you to act impulsively. The last thing he can afford is for you to start thinking things through.

150. If you feel that you are being manipulated, you probably are. Trust your gut instincts. When something doesn't feel right, do not act. Pause. Ask questions.

151. The sycophant subordinate smothers you in praise and admiration. Well, this is fine—whether the compliments are sincere or not—as long as you don't let the flattering talk interfere with making assignments and assessing performance. If necessary, cut through the florid verbiage politely but firmly: "Jane, I'm glad you appreciate what I'm trying to do. Now, let's get down to working out your overtime schedule."

SURVIVING

THE STUBBORN

152. First, try facts. Often, the only thing harder than a hard-headed supervisor or colleague is a hard fact. You are trying to get your boss to consider doing business with a new vendor. He responds: "I just don't like Acme widgets. I intend to stick with Smith Brand. And that's it." *You:* "Have you seen the report in *Widget Weekly* comparing Acme and Smith? It shows a 15 percent increase in torque with Acme—and at a 10 percent cost saving!"

153. Find superiority in numbers. Butting one head against another can be a fruitless enterprise. Assemble a coalition. Talk up a project or idea among colleagues and coworkers. Build up a "market" for it. Then make your presentation: "Caroline, I've run this by *everybody* in sales, and they all see it as a winner. I've jotted down a few of their remarks. Do you want to take a look?"

154. "Damn the torpedoes! Four bells, Captain Drayton, go ahead!" When Union Admiral David Farragut gave this order at the Battle of Mobile Bay, he became a Civil War hero. Of course, had his ship hit a "torpedo" (that's what they called mines back then), he'd have been dead—and so would a lot of U.S. sailors. Farragut got lucky and gained a victory, but what do you do when your boss sails *you* into a mine field? Arguing and accusing won't do any good at all. It might even make him even more determined to stay the course. The first thing to try is repeating the boss's crazy plan back to him: "Let me make sure that I understand. You want to . . ." Perhaps hearing his own orders— as rephrased by you—will serve as the splash of cold water in the face needed to wake him up.

155. When you are given an unworkable order, don't argue. Agree with what you can, but suggest some alternatives: "I'm glad we're going to go after that segment of the market. Seems like a great idea. My only suggestion is that we begin with a test first . . ."

156. If you run up against a brick wall—you are given an assignment with "disaster" written all over it, your boss won't take no for an answer, and she won't listen to the alternatives you propose—at least get the order in writing. If necessary, you should prepare a memo detailing the assignment and get your boss to sign off on it. In this way you'll have some measure of protection when the stupid deal falls apart.

157. Colleagues can be as unbending as bosses. When a coworker is set in his ways about how something should be done, it can be difficult to get him to change—even if change is clearly beneficial or necessary. You can try to adhere to the facts and the issues, presenting evidence as to why proposition B is superior to proposition A, or you can try to find some middle ground in order to get your colleague to bend at least a few degrees: "Mary, I don't think we're too far apart on this. Look, we agree on A, B, and C, and we disagree only on D. Can we at least implement three of the four proposed stages?"

158. Some people are too proud to speak up when they need help. Stubbornly, they will try to do an assigned task, muck it up beyond all recognition, then never say a word. Don't wait for this to happen. When you assign an employee a new task, ask her if she has any questions. Ask if she feels comfortable with the assignment. Make it perfectly clear that it is all right to ask questions. Finally, be certain that all of your instructions are absolutely explicit and that they have been understood.

159. A customer places an order. You know that she has ordered an item that is inappropriate for the application she has in mind for it. You tell her this. She stubbornly insists that she is ordering what she wants. Do you make the sale, knowing that, sooner or later, the customer will come back dissatisfied? Or do you continue to argue with her—and risk losing a sale, as well as alienating a customer? The better alternative is to be patient and explain that, of course, you will sell her whatever she wants, but you are less concerned about making a sale than you are about ensuring that you have made a satisfied customer: "Ms. Smith, of course I'll sell you widget A. I'm in business to sell widgets. But I am less interested in making a sale than in making sure that you are absolutely satisfied. And I have to tell you, I do not think that you will be happy with the performance widget A—not if you want to use it for application B. Have you given any thought to widget B? Would you like me to tell you about it?"

160. Rigid behavior may take the form of a determination to be miserable and to make everyone else in the vicinity miserable. The idea is that you are all being paid to work, not to have anything resembling a good time. If you're stuck with a stubborn killjoy, try being friendly. Don't isolate him. Engage him in small talk. Invite him to lunch. Be patient, and don't push. Integrate him gradually into office "society."

161. No one is more stubborn than a person in a rut. Try to get one of these colleagues or supervisors to move beyond the status quo, and she will probably quote you chapter and verse from a policies and procedures manual. In dealing with a worshiper of the way-things-are, first be certain that you are not bending the rules for the sake of bending them, but that the situation really does demand moving beyond the usual and customary. Appeal to the person's sense of order and organization: "Bill, we need to reorganize for this project. You have such a thorough knowledge of how the system works, your input would be invaluable for this project. Would you help us out?"

NEUTRALIZING MORALE BUSTERS

162. The workplace should be a civil place. It's not a church, to be sure, but it should be a place where one can expect to function without being insulted, abused, threatened, or made to feel uncomfortable. Sometimes, however, the pressure builds up, and employees will argue with one another—usually at considerable volume and with a vocabulary of choice words. Anger and irritation are understandable, but they cannot be allowed to disrupt the workplace. If loud, harsh, unpleasant disputes become the norm, you will find yourself laboring in a chronically hostile environment. Cope with disputes not by volunteering as referee between two bellowing subordinates. Instead, separate them, and speak to each individually. Persuade them—individually—that they must work together to resolve their differences.

163. Communicate with each hothead in three steps. First, acknowledge the person's anger: "You are obviously very angry." Next, ask questions: "What is upsetting you?" Keep responding to the hothead's explanations. Mirror them. *Hothead:* "Nobody has any respect for me." *You:* "You believe we don't respect you?" *Hothead:* "That's right. I never get listened to around here." *You:* "Your ideas aren't appreciated?" Finally, after you have given the hothead a chance to vent, to express himself, and to cool off, make it clear that you will not tolerate further angry outbursts: "Bob, we'll work together to try to change some things around here. But, in the meantime, you have to understand that I won't tolerate abusive, high-volume language here. It's not fair to the rest of us. It is simply unacceptable."

164. In any organization, informal subgroups are formed, and people gather about them their own personal set of friends and associates. Nothing wrong with that—until cliques become conspiratorial, gossip-generating, grumbling gangs that undermine your authority and cut into productivity. You need to take action. Often, the most effective move you can make is to identify the ringleader and win him over to your side. Empower him. Give him special assignments. Keep him close to you. Get him to plan with you rather than conspire with his clique.

165. You may want to break up cliques by empowering individual members and winning them over to your side through mentoring, encouragement, and generally improved communication. If possible, offer material incentives as well: bonuses for special achievements, extra vacation, opportunities for advancement, and so on.

166. Cliques can be dissolved by reassigning personnel, moving them to other divisions, assigning them different hours, or giving them separate tasks unrelated to one another.

167. Try exploiting cliques rather than obliterating them. If you look at the clique as a group of people who get along well and like each other, maybe they will also work together well. Assign the group special projects. In effect, institutionalize the clique—make it an "official" team.

168. Seems childish, doesn't it? The snitch. The tattletale. The worker who habitually comes to you with gossip about others. Staying alert and sensitive to problems employees may be having is important to effective management, but you never want to give the impression that you rely on snitches or that you have a network of spies to keep tabs on your department. Such feelings poison your shop and quickly dissolve morale. The next time gossip about somebody's "problem" is delivered to you, explain your position politely but firmly: "Max, I appreciate your sensitivity to Brenda's situation. But I think it best if we let Brenda work it out herself. She knows that she can come and talk to me if she wants to. Let's be discreet. I don't want to turn this place into a gossip mill. Let's just leave her alone. Do we understand one another?"

169. Internet, intranet, network, inter-office mail, the telephone—all great means of communicating information. But nothing is faster or more efficient than the grapevine and the rumor mill. Unfortunately, it is also true that few things are more destructive to office morale. Morale is built on perception, and once rumors get started, you lose your handle on subordinates' perception—of you, of the business, of your organization, of one another. It will do little good to issue an edict forbidding rumors—though you *should* take this step, making it clear that discretion is important in your business and that rumor mongering is therefore destructive. In addition to this necessary but (let's face it) relatively ineffectual *official* step, make it your business to keep your door open. Invite the rumor monger to talk directly to you. Get her story, make corrections, and send her back out with the "true facts." If you encounter a disturbing rumor, question the tale bearer thoroughly. Find out her sources. Determine how reliable the rumor is.

170   There is one very simple way of dealing with rumors. Cut them short. If what you are hearing is obviously mere spiteful and unfounded gossip, walk away. "Bob, I just don't want to hear that." You'll make your point.

171.   Every office has its curmudgeons and bearers of doom and gloom. The First Amendment to the Constitution notwithstanding, gloomy talk is contagious and should be stopped. Confront the habitual harbinger of doom: "Dolores, I am concerned that your negative assessment of the Baker project is affecting morale and performance here. You know, your opinions may be rather more sophisticated than some of the junior people can handle. If they begin to feel bad about the account, their feelings may start to make themselves evident in their work. I don't want that to happen. Please confine your doubts to conversations with me. Air them in senior management meetings, by all means. But, please, let's not give the non-management staff more misery than they can understand or handle. I would really appreciate your cooperation."

TACKLING THE
TACITURN

172. Working for an aloof and uncommunicative boss can be emotionally trying and, even worse, can lead to misunderstandings and mistakes. You begin to feel that you're just not very important to the man. And because he makes it so difficult to talk with him, you avoid communicating altogether, even when the job demands it. The first step is to fight your growing inertia. Force yourself to keep the lines of communication open. Find things to say that will make the boss feel good. Give him news that he will want to hear: "Good morning, Mr. Witherspoon. Did you catch the *Journal* article on widget market expansion? It looks like our timing is just right!"

173. Make communication as easy for the boss as possible. Don't load her down with overly detailed reports and useless FYI information. Design sharp, concise executive summaries that highlight key information: "Gloria, I've prepared an executive summary of the Peabody report. Of course, I've got the backup data, if you need to see it."

174. Some bosses are *selectively* uncommunicative. Not aloof by nature, they nevertheless clam up and fail to react when you make a key proposal. Such an instance may become a minor battle of wills. If your presentation meets with stony silence, ask questions—open-ended questions that require more than a yes or no: "What else can I tell you about X?"

175. Silence, as you may become painfully aware, is a powerful tool. So why not use it yourself? If you fail to get a response from your boss, don't move. Wait. Smile. Wait some more. Let the silence get uncomfortable.

176. At some point, silence can become too uncomfortable. Give yourself and your boss an out: "Ms. Harris, I assume from your silence that I haven't given you everything you need to make a decision. What more can I tell you? What other information would you like me to get?"

177. Silence is not the only way to avoid communication. You ask a straightforward question—only to receive an evasive non-answer. Don't let go: "Mr. Victor, is there some reason you won't answer me on this? Have I done something wrong? Is there more information you need from me?" Appeal to mutual interest: "Mr. Victor, you know that we both want to cut costs. But I can't start moving toward that goal without answers to these basic questions."

178. Colleagues can sometimes withhold information for apparently capricious reasons, or, perhaps, to maintain a feeling of control ("I know something you don't know!"). You'd like to shake the information you need right out of these people. But the more effective approach is to swallow hard, take a deep breath, and turn on the charm: "Mary Lou, I don't know what we'd do without you and your sampling data. I know that you usually don't issue a report until the tenth, but I really need the information now. You do such a great job of putting this material together."

179. Maybe your colleague is being uncommunicative because he just doesn't feel ready to share his work. This is especially likely when you are dealing with perfectionists. In this case, express understanding and respect for his professionalism: "Peter, I understand that you're not thrilled about circulating an unrevised draft. I respect that. But I just need to get an idea of the direction of your data, so that I don't end up reinventing the wheel or duplicating what you've already done. I'll keep your work in confidence. We're all looking forward to reading your final report when you are ready to present it."

180. A colleague's silence may be an expression of anger. If you suspect this to be the case, your best strategy is to get the problem out into the open so that it can be discussed and resolved. Letting it simmer is not a viable option. "Melinda, you tell me that nothing is wrong, but that's about *all* you say to me these days. Now, we've had an honest and productive relationship. I don't think we've ever had trouble communicating before. Go ahead. Tell me what's going on here." Caution: Before you take this approach, make certain that you are willing to deal rationally and calmly with whatever grievances your colleague may finally air. Nothing is less productive than asking for honesty, only to react to it with outrage.

181. Believe it or not, those who report to you may have trouble expressing themselves. They may be shy, embarrassed, intimidated—afraid that what they have to say isn't worth your time and attention. Bring these folks out of their shells with gentle reassurance and direct questions prefaced by encouragement: "Jane, I always enjoy hearing from you on sales matters. Tell me, how would you boost the widget line?"

FUNCTIONING

WITH

FAULT-FINDERS

182. Fault finders are irritating, that's for sure. The single best way to foil them is to avoid fault in the first place. Take pride in what you do. Check and double check your work. Make it hard for anyone to find a problem with it.

183. Don't necessarily shun fault finders. Don't evade them. Thank them for their help: "Karl, I sure appreciate your input on project X. Your comments helped me to improve the output considerably. I appreciate it."

184. Some fault finders will find fault even when there is absolutely nothing wrong. You want to wring their necks, but, instead, just avoid issues of personality and address the work. Ask the fault finder for specifics: "Jill, can you tell me exactly where you find the problem? I just don't understand. As far as I can see, it all checks out fine."

185. Yield something to the fault finder. This may well steal his thunder. The fault finder is looking to get a rise out of you, to put you on the defensive. Instead, practice humility: "You know, Ron, you're right, this unit *isn't* perfect. We've upped productivity by 14 percent, but we've still got a long way to go. I hope that you'll draw up a list of suggestions I can review."

186. Some fault finders rush to judgment before gathering all the facts. Your first impulse is to panic and become enraged over the injustice. But stay calm. Snap judgments mean jumping the gun. They are about acting without thinking. It's up to you to respond with calm rationality: "Boss, I can understand why you would blame me for this. You don't have all the information you need. Let me fill you in."

187. In the name of honesty, some folks can be sadistically brutal. They will rip you to shreds: "Look, I have to be honest. This is the worst presentation I have ever seen! If I sat up all night trying to think of what not to do, I couldn't have come up with something *this* bad!" The hardest thing you have to do is keep from caving in under the attack. Blunt its impact by asking for specifics. However, stand your ground, and do not concede anything. Instead, acknowledge the attack as an opinion—not fact: "Jack, I see that you have strong feelings about the presentation. Can you be more specific about them?" Jack answers: "No! I mean, where could I possibly begin?" You respond: "Well, just hearing your opinion is not very helpful. I need real criticism—detail, concrete suggestions."

188. Colleagues and subordinates who make it their business to find fault can quickly undermine morale. Squelch habitual fault finders not by avoiding them, but by staying closely in touch with them. Keep them informed. Solicit their reactions. When they find fault, probe. Probe deeply. Insist on explanations for their judgments. Two things are likely to happen. First, the frequency of the fault finding will be reduced; you've made it too much like real work. Second, you might actually obtain *valuable* criticism, detailed enough to help you to improve a product, a process, or performance.

189. Sarcasm is another variety of fault finding. We've all known the office cynic who dismisses any effort out of hand: "Oh, Bill's got another 'brainstorm.' Look out!" Don't let this pass. Intervene— but don't direct attention to the mocker. Instead, focus on the effort or the person under attack: "I always look forward to these 'brainstorms,' because they've produced some pretty productive ideas—like the wonder widget. We've done quite nicely with that."

190. If you are the target of a sarcastic dismissal, disarm the attacker by using his own weapon. *Mocker:* "Sarah, is this another one of your 'brainstorms'?" *You:* "That's right. Better break out the umbrellas—'cause it's about to come down on *you!*" Take the sarcasm in stride, and use it to kid yourself. Show that it is absolutely harmless.

191. Subordinates have a right to complain, and, if you listen carefully, you might be able to make changes that will improve conditions for everybody. But there is a difference between an intelligent complaint and a piercing whine. Whiners protest the relatively unimportant: "Why can't we get decent coffee in the break room? What kind of cheapo outfit is this, anyway?" If you can, assign a problem-solving task to the whiner: "Muriel, I'm not crazy about the coffee, either. I'd like you to do some research on alternatives to the coffee we're getting now. Please prepare an informal report by Tuesday. We'll try to act on your recommendation."

192. You're P.O.'d. *Really* P.O.'d. There's someone at work who annoys you to no end. In fact, that's why you bought this book. You are not alone. Plenty of people find themselves in this situation. How do you manage your frustration? One way is to refuse to let the problem person become an obsession. Get around him. Keep busy. Focus on work. Focus on issues. Focus on the people you do get along with. If you spend any number of waking hours thinking about your nemesis and the problems he creates, you are inadvertently allowing him to control you. Big mistake.

CREATIVE
VENTING

193. Talk with friends. Sometimes talking out problems with personal friends or loved ones helps a great deal. Don't just complain, however. Really talk a problem through. You will want to be more cautious about consulting friends at work, lest you appear to be a gossip. Also, unless you are absolutely sure you can trust your work friend, you never know how information may come back to haunt you.

194. Count to 20. It really works—if you can remember to do it. Sometimes a mere 20 seconds is the only thing separating you from a steady job and the unemployment line. Give yourself some time to cool off and compose yourself when you really feel that the heat is on.

195. Take a walk. Get a fresh perspective beyond your four walls. Being cooped up in an office can put anyone on edge. Not only will a change of scene help clear your mind, getting outdoors and breathing fresh air will wake you up and energize you.

196. Make a list—at home!—of your work gripes. Call it your gripe diary. Make sure you're honest. "I am mad at my boss because he's over-critical, uncaring, and egotistical." Putting emotions into words on paper (or a computer screen) can help you see what the root problems are. The list can also help you acknowledge your feelings. Just don't show it to anyone at work.

197. Pour yourself into your work. It may only be a temporary solution, but one of the best revenges against those who tick you off is to succeed wildly well at what you do. While there are few prizes given out for complaining about other people, there are quite a few rewards for hard work. Temporary workaholism should not be a substitute for addressing the root problems, but it is better than complaining or just plain stewing.

198. Create a time and a place for venting. If your company does not already have one, create a suggestion/complaint box. Consider the option of anonymous complaints.

199. Designate someone on your staff to act as an ombudsman. Perhaps someone from human resources could serve—though you might find it more effective to nominate a representative from your own department. The ombudsman should be empowered either to take action or, at least, to communicate directly with those in authority.

200. Encourage an open exchange early. At meetings, for example, intercede as soon as you see a problem developing. "Now, before we move on to the next item, I want to touch on something Jim said. Clearly, you disagree with Marsha on point so-and-so. I hope we can clear this up now, and, after we've resolved the issue, move on." You can act as a mediator between two potential rivals by encouraging them to put their cards on the table. This takes skill and practice, but it can help defuse potential problems.

201. If it appears that a stubborn minority just won't give in you can always table the issue, then ask the dissenter to prepare something clearly stating their perspective and their proposed alternative course of action. At the next meeting, the minority view can be considered and put to a vote that everyone must respect.